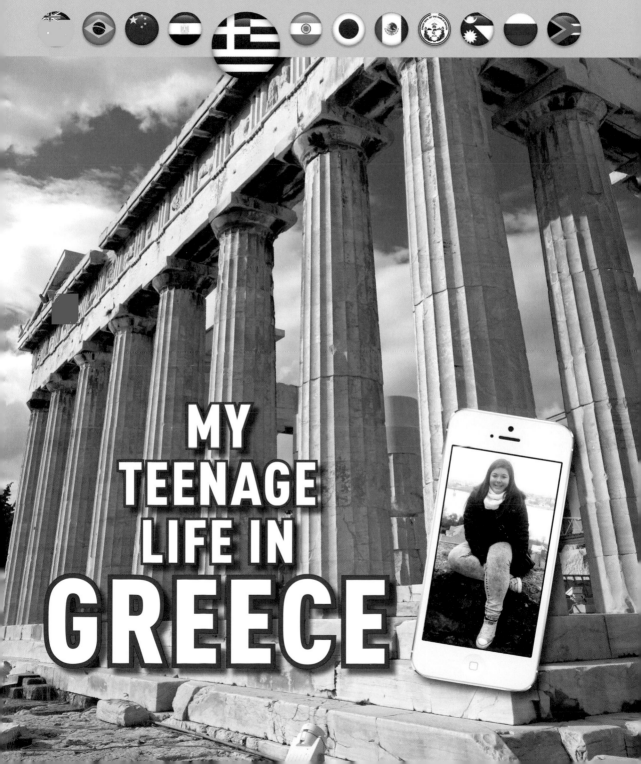

CUSTOMS AND CULTURES OF THE WORLD

MY TEENAGE LIFE IN GREECE

CUSTOMS AND CULTURES OF THE WORLD

My Teenage Life in AUSTRALIA

My Teenage Life in BRAZIL

My Teenage Life in CHINA

My Teenage Life in EGYPT

My Teenage Life in GREECE

My Teenage Life in INDIA

My Teenage Life in JAPAN

My Teenage Life in MEXICO

My Teenage Life in NEPAL

My Teenage Life in RUSSIA

My Teenage Life in SOUTH AFRICA

Our Teenage Life in the NAVAJO NATION

CUSTOMS AND CULTURES OF THE WORLD

MY TEENAGE LIFE IN GREECE

By James Buckley Jr.
with Hara Adam

Series Foreword by
Kum-Kum Bhavnani

Mason Crest
450 Parkway Drive, Suite D
Broomall, PA 19008
www.masoncrest.com

© 2018 by Mason Crest, an imprint of National Highlights, Inc.

Printed and bound in the United States of America.

First printing
9 8 7 6 5 4 3 2 1

Series ISBN: 978-1-4222-3899-8
ISBN: 978-1-4222-3904-9
ebook ISBN: 978-1-4222-7883-3

Library of Congress Cataloging-in-Publication Data on file with the publisher.

Developed and Produced by Shoreline Publishing Group.
Editor: James Buckley, Jr.
Design: Tom Carling, Carling Design Inc.
Production: Sandy Gordon
www.shorelinepublishing.com

Front cover: Dreamstime.com/bcbounders

QR Codes disclaimer:

 GREECE

CONTENTS

Key Icons to Look For

 Words to Understand: These words with their easy-to-understand definitions will increase the reader's understanding of the text, while building vocabulary skills.

 Sidebars: This boxed material within the main text allows readers to build knowledge, gain insights, explore possibilities, and broaden their perspectives by weaving together additional information to provide realistic and holistic perspectives.

 Educational Videos: Readers can view videos by scanning our QR codes, providing them with additional educational content to supplement the text. Examples include news coverage, moments in history, speeches, iconic sports moments, and much more!

 Text-Dependent Questions: These questions send the reader back to the text for more careful attention to the evidence presented here.

 Research Projects: Readers are pointed toward areas of further inquiry connected to each chapter. Suggestions are provided for projects that encourage deeper research and analysis.

Series Glossary of Key Terms: This back-of-the-book glossary contains terminology used throughout this series. Words found here increase the reader's ability to read and comprehend higher-level books and articles in this field.

SERIES FOREWORD

Culture:
Parts = Whole

Culture makes us human. Many of us think of culture as something that belongs to a person, a group, or even a country. We talk about the food of a region as being part of its culture (tacos, pupusas, tamales, and burritos all are part of our understanding of food from Mexico, and South and Central America).

We might also talk about the clothes as being important to culture (saris in India, kimonos in Japan, hijabs or *gallibayas* in Egypt, or beaded shirts in the Navajo Nation). Imagine trying to sum up "American" culture using just examples like these! Yet culture does not just belong to a person or even a country. It is not only about food and clothes or music and art, because those things by themselves cannot tell the whole story.

Culture is also about how we live our lives. It is about our lived experiences of our societies and of all the worlds we inhabit. And in this series—Customs and Cultures of the World—you will meet young people who will share their experiences of the cultures and worlds they inhabit.

How does a teenager growing up in South Africa make sense of the history of apartheid, the 1994 democratic elections, and of what is happening now? That is as integral to our world's culture as the ancient ruins in Greece, the pyramids of Egypt, the Great Wall of China, the Himalayas above Nepal, and the Amazon rain forests in Brazil.

But these examples are not enough. Greece is also known for its financial uncertainties, Egypt is known for the uprisings in Tahrir Square, China is known for its rapid development of megacities, Australia is known for its amazing animals, and Brazil is known for the Olympics and its football [soccer] team. And there are many more examples for each nation, region, and person, and some of these examples are featured in these books. The question is: How do you, growing up in a particular country, view your own culture? What do you think of as culture? What is your lived experience of it? How do you come to understand and engage with cultures that are not familiar to you? And, perhaps most importantly, why do you/we want to do this? And how does reading about and experiencing other cultures help you understand your own?

It is perhaps a cliché to say culture forms the central core of our humanity and our dignity. If that's true, how do young adults talk about your own cultures? How do you simultaneously understand how people apparently "different" from you live their lives, and engage

with their cultures? One way is to read the stories in this series. The "authors" are just like you, even though they live in different places and in different cultures. We communicated with these young writers over the Internet, which has become the greatest gathering of cultures ever. The Internet is now central to the culture of almost everyone, with young people leading the way on how to use it to expand the horizons of all of us. From those of us born in earlier generations, thank you for opening that cultural avenue!

Let me finish by saying that culture allows us to open our minds, think about worlds different from the ones we live in, and to imagine how people very different from us live their lives. This series of books is just the start of the process, but a crucial start.

I hope you enjoy them.

—Kum-Kum Bhavnani
Professor of sociology and feminist and global studies at the University of California, Santa Barbara, and an award-winning international filmmaker.

GREECE

MEET HARA!

My name is Hara Adam. I am 16 years old and live with my family in Thessaloniki, the second-largest city in Greece. I am in the third year grade of high school, which is the senior one.

MY NAME IN GREEK!
Χαρά Αδάμ

I have an older brother. His name is Pashalis and he is 19. He is a student at the University of Macedonia at the Economics department.

My dad, Themistoklis, is in charge of a company's warehouse and he also does delivery at a pizza restaurant.

My mom, Anastasia, is head of the accounting department at a windscreen company. (That's what we call the glass on the front of a car…you say "windshield.")

MEET HARA

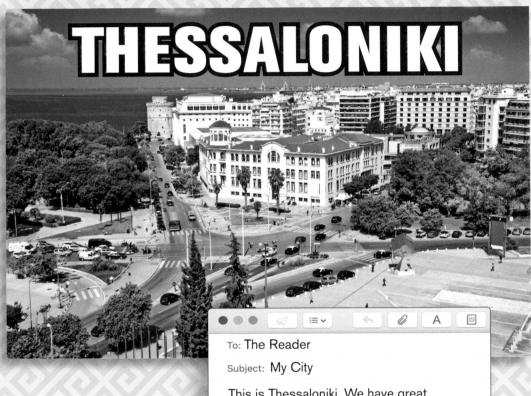

THESSALONIKI

To: The Reader

Subject: My City

This is Thessaloniki. We have great beaches in this area, but the only problem with [where I live in] Thessaloniki is that it's a long way to the beach. We have to take at least two buses to go to the beach because we don't have any that are very close to us. In the summer, there is a bus that takes us to a beach bar and drives you back, but it takes forever to take one 'cause it's always full!

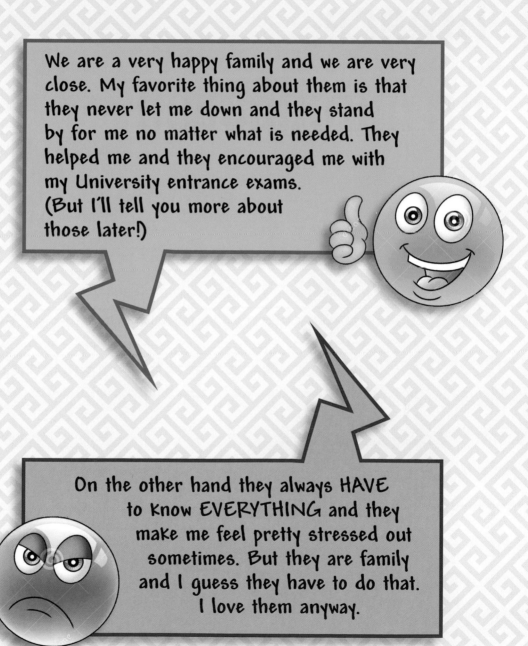

We are a very happy family and we are very close. My favorite thing about them is that they never let me down and they stand by for me no matter what is needed. They helped me and they encouraged me with my University entrance exams.
(But I'll tell you more about those later!)

On the other hand they always HAVE to know EVERYTHING and they make me feel pretty stressed out sometimes. But they are family and I guess they have to do that. I love them anyway.

Greece: An Introduction

The history of Greece stretches back to ancient times, making it one of the world's oldest civilizations. Lately, however, the country has been acting in some ways like it's just getting started.

The nation of Greece is in southern Europe. It's a large peninsula stretching into the Mediterranean Sea and also includes a large number of islands to the east and west of the peninsula. Home to nearly 11 million people, Greece includes large cities such as its capital, Athens, but also large, lightly populated mountain areas. Farming remains a key part of life for many small towns and villages, but the areas near the coast have become hugely popular tourist destinations. The islands dotting the Aegean and Ionian Seas to the east and west are especially well known for their white beaches and seaside attractions.

Today's Greece lives amid the signs and remains of thousands of years of history and of a people whose impact became worldwide.

Words to Understand

resonate   echo and reverberate; stay current through time

tyrannies   governments run by the total rule of one person

Remains of ancient Roman influence on Greece can be seen throughout the country, such as this Galerius arch in Hara's hometown of Thessaloniki.

Ancient Greece

What is Greece today began as a collection of villages that slowly gathered themselves together into city-states. These city-states were run in a variety of ways, from kingdoms to outright **tyrannies**. However, one of them, Athens, eventually used a new form of government it called democracy, which in the Greek language of the time meant "rule by the people."(Of course, that was a loose definition. Women did not have votes, nor did all the men. Only a group of land-owning "citizens" earned the right to vote. And

Athens also had tens of thousands of slaves at work in the city.) The idea of people voting for their interests and of a majority of those votes creating the outcome was a new one. For a time, Athens was a mighty city, home to great philosophers, architects, artists, and leaders. These Athenians built the famous building called the Parthenon that still dominates the heights above Athens. They had a powerful navy and took advantage of the area's many natural resources and farmland.

Other city-states, however, were not as enlightened, and the Peloponnesian Wars in the 400s BCE among the city-states opened the door for another, larger kingdom to invade. The war is named for the peninsula upon which the Greek city-states were mostly located. The kingdom of Macedon to the north eventually took over most of what is now Greece, led first by King Philip II and later by his son, the famed conqueror Alexander the Great. Because of this, the Athenian experiment of representative democracy was short-lived.

Though Alexander ruled the Greek world during his lifetime, he was inspired by it as well. One of his teachers was the famed philosopher Aristotle, who in turn had been taught by Plato (PLAY-toh). Other famed Greek philosophers of this period include Socrates, Diogenes, and Pythagoras.

Under Other's Orders

After the death of Alexander in 323 BCE, the Greek city-states slowly came under the control of the much larger Roman Empire. The Romans took the area over completely after defeating Greek forces in Corinth in

146 BCE. Based in Rome, the Empire came to dominate much of Europe and North Africa over the coming centuries. But as much as the Romans exerted their control over the people and the lands, they also soaked up the vibrant Greek culture.

Like Alexander, the Romans, and later, most of the Western world were greatly influenced by the philosophy of the ancient Greeks. Their thoughts on the nature of man and his place in the world, about science and its relationship to humanity, and about the ideas of consciousness and being have **resonated** through the centuries. Their writings are still a key part of many philosophy, science, and history classes.

Roman writers and thinkers were greatly influenced and inspired by Greeks, including Virgil, who wrote the epic poem called *The Aeneid* after reading works by the Greek writer Homer (author of *The Odyssey* and *The Iliad*, stories of even older Greek wars and heroes). Roman emperors often visited Athens and other Greek cities and even paid for new buildings to be created in the various Greek styles.

Though they were under the thumb of the Roman Empire, the Greeks did enjoy

Alexander the Great played a big part in making Greece a leader in the Mediterranean world.

the longest stretch without war in their history to that point. The power of the Roman Empire was such that no one really dared oppose it and the period until the fourth century was known as the Pax Romana, or Roman Peace.

That era finally ended when the massive Roman Empire split in two in 324. The emperor Constantine set up an Eastern or "Byzantine" Roman Empire with a capital in Constantinople, the city that is now Istanbul, Turkey. The Greeks fell under the control of the Byzantine Empire, which stayed mostly whole even as the Western half of the Roman Empire fell to invading European tribes in the 400s and 500s.

The Byzantine Empire itself fell in 1204 at the hands of invaders from what is now France and Germany. The lands changed hands again when the Ottoman Turks, invading Muslim forces from the south and east, took over and ruled Greece for nearly 500 years. During this time, the Sultans who ran the Ottoman Empire relied on the leader of the Orthodox Christian Church, called the Patriarch, to help keep the Greek people in line. To maintain the ability to practice the religion (see the chapter on Greek Culture), the Orthodox Church played a huge

This mosaic is typical of the artwork inspired by the Byzantine Empire.

Greek soldiers take part in the annual Independence Day parade, which celebrates modern Greece's separation from the Ottoman Empire in 1821.

role in schools and other institutions. Heavy taxes on all the people and their businesses also meant that few Greeks were able to build up the fortunes of years past, although those in the shipping trade did very well.

Throughout all this domination, the Greek people maintained most of their language, culture, and spirit, which would serve them well in the difficult years ahead.

From Empire to Independence

As the Ottoman Empire slowly collapsed in the 1700s and early 1800s, the collection of city-states in Greece saw an opening. They banded together and declared their independence from the Ottomans in 1821. With backing from other European powers, they were able to split and create the new nation of Greece in 1830. While they retained some of the original ideas

The end of World War II was a joyous time in Greece, as Allied forces chased out the invaders from Nazi Germany, opening the way for a new Greek government.

of democracy, they did choose to elect a king to rule them. In 1832, they found a prince from German Bavaria named Otto to take charge. Over the coming decades, Greece added lands and islands to the nation.

In the 1920s, they voted to oust the royalty and become a republic, but that lasted only about a decade. In the early 1940s, Greece was once again under the control of an outside power, as Nazi Germany invaded and held the nation throughout World War II. With the end of the war came another opportunity to create a truly modern Greek state. In 1952, the country finally created a constitution, though it chose to retain a king while also creating a parliamentary democracy.

Following the takeover of the country in 1967 by a group of generals in what is known as a coup, a lasting independence began in 1973. Since then, although there has been a series of struggles and crises, the country has been run, ideally, as the kind of people-centered democracy to which the ancient Athenians aspired.

However, as shown in the Economy and Politics chapter, in recent years, the success of the leaders of today's Greece will not inspire future generations as much as their ancient forebears did. Starting in 2007 and 2008, Greece faced enormous economic difficulties brought on partly by poor decisions by the national government amid a growing international recession. The problems worsened dramatically in 2015 and forward, leading to a near-collapse of the Greek economy. Only help from outside, including the European Union and the World Bank, staved off a real disaster. Even then, many Greeks faced serious hardships and the country is still far from recovered. Whether Greece can rebound will be one of the key stories in Europe in the coming years. ✳

Greek history

HARA'S SCHOOL LIFE

My Schedule

Start Class: 8:15 am

First Class: 30 minutes

Second through Sixth Class: 45 minutes each

Seventh Class: 30 minutes

Day Over (Finally!): 2:05

Here's my school, it's called the First High School of Echedoros, which is the name of the neighborhood it's in. Most of the kids here have known each other since kindergarten or primary school.

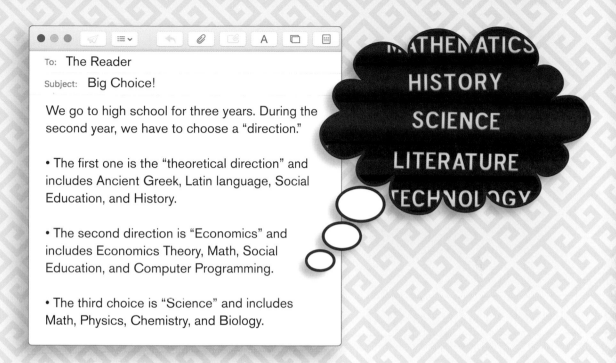

To: The Reader

Subject: Big Choice!

We go to high school for three years. During the second year, we have to choose a "direction."

• The first one is the "theoretical direction" and includes Ancient Greek, Latin language, Social Education, and History.

• The second direction is "Economics" and includes Economics Theory, Math, Social Education, and Computer Programming.

• The third choice is "Science" and includes Math, Physics, Chemistry, and Biology.

MATHEMATICS
HISTORY
SCIENCE
LITERATURE
TECHNOLOGY

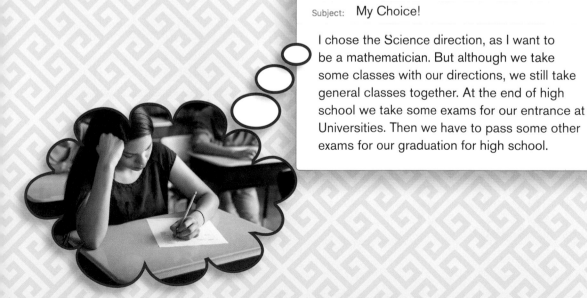

To: The Reader

Subject: My Choice!

I chose the Science direction, as I want to be a mathematician. But although we take some classes with our directions, we still take general classes together. At the end of high school we take some exams for our entrance at Universities. Then we have to pass some other exams for our graduation for high school.

HARA'S SCHOOL LIFE

 New Post

 Hara Adams
My School Life
Like • Comment • Share

Math Rules!: My favorite subject is Math. I just love it. I think that if you can understand math you can understand much more about the world and the universe. I think I see things more different than many kids my age, who don't understand that way of thought. I think you NEED to be able to understand Math.

Modern History... mehhh!: My least favorite subject is Modern History. I just get so bored in class. And it's not about the teacher...our teacher is GREAT, but the subject...mehhh!

From Bad to Good: I love to read but I hate school. Sincerely, my early school years were the worst in my life. From primary school until the first year of high school! It was very difficult for me to make friends since I was bullied at primary school. Bullying is a very bad thing, not only in Greece but globally. But in my first year of high school, I actually made friends that year, like my friend Ava. We spend a lot of time together during our breaks from class.

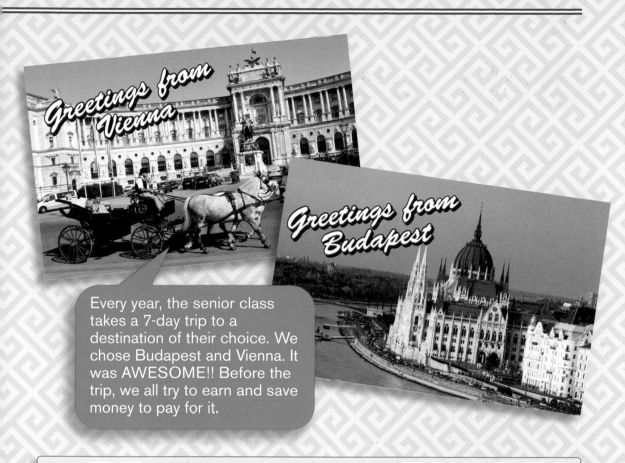

Every year, the senior class takes a 7-day trip to a destination of their choice. We chose Budapest and Vienna. It was AWESOME!! Before the trip, we all try to earn and save money to pay for it.

To: The Reader

Subject: Family Prom

Every year around Christmas, our school plans a family prom to raise money and to kind of say goodbye to school, and this year it was beautiful. We made a video with our photos from our childhood and our puberty, we made a song about our teachers, we made a theater performance and we showed it . . . I think it was very unique and that's why it will be my best memory from my school years.

 GREECE

Greek Customs

As a nation founded on a collection of city-states, Greece has many regional customs, particular to a location. However, the country has over the centuries created numerous national customs shared by Greeks from all over.

Tied to the Church

The Greek Orthodox Christian Church is the source of most Greek customs. It grew out of the Eastern Orthodox Church that was the religion of the Byzantine Empire. Nearly every Greek family belongs to or has roots in the church. While participation in weekly services certainly varies, religious holidays throughout the calendar serve to define the year and are celebrated annually by nearly everyone in some form or another.

The period of carnival that precedes Lent is known as *Apokries*, which means "goodbyes." It is the last time that the **Orthodox** faithful will enjoy themselves completely before beginning the fasting and rituals of

Words to Understand

Epiphany   a Christian holiday marking 12 days after Christmas and the day that, according to the Bible, the three kings visited and began to believe in the divinity of the baby Jesus

Orthodox   part of the name of a major Christian denomination; as a word, it means "sticking to what is generally accepted to be right and correct"

A Greek Orthodox priest offers blessings to the faithful during one of the many services related to the Easter holiday.

Lent, the time leading up to Easter. The final days include *Tsiknopempti*, the last day of being able to eat whatever meat you want. (During Lent, many Christians abstain from beef on Fridays.) *Tyrofagos* is the last day of the pre-Lent period, and is a day for feasting on cheese. Finally, the Monday before Lent begins is called Clean Monday; many families enjoy a holiday on this day.

Hara on Faith

My family is Christian Orthodox, except me. I don't believe in anything; you can call me an atheist. I like to have proof of my beliefs. I cannot believe in something I can't see. Anyway, religion is very important for the people of Greece. My family members, even though they like going to church, they sometimes don't have time or the energy. On holidays they usually go, however.

I may not believe, but I don't underestimate other religions. I think that anyone is free to believe in any God or theory he wants. In my country, most of the people are Orthodox but also there are people who are Muslims and Jehovah's Witnesses.

Easter is the most important event, as it is in most Christian traditions. The days leading up to the holiday are known as Holy Week, and each day includes particular events. Holy Thursday, for instance, is when families make special cakes called tsourekia. They also color eggs, with red being the dominant color. On Good Friday, processions are often held to honor the death of Jesus.

As with other areas of Greek customs, there are regional variations. In Corfu, for example, clay pots are tossed from windows on Holy Saturday. The broken pieces symbolize how, with Easter, a Christian is made whole again.

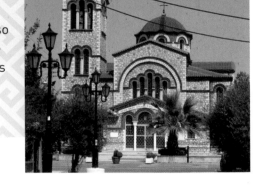

Christmas also creates some well-known Greek traditions. The Orthodox Church celebrates the 12 days of Christmas, and the **Epiphany** holiday is the ending celebration. Along the coasts and amid the many islands, young men dive into the sea at Ephiphany. They are seeking a crucifix that a priest has thrown in the water. The lucky diver who finds the cross receives an extra blessing. Another Christmas tradition is the singing of songs called *kalanda*. Much like

Christmas carols in other lands, these are songs sung by groups of neighbors to each other. Many families make and cut a cake called *vasilopita*, which has a coin hidden inside. Whoever finds the coin in his or her piece is lucky for a year. They cut the cake in honor of Saint Vassilios (also called Saint Basil in English). And while other traditions include Christmas elves, in Greece, they are known as *kallikantzari* and are said to create mischief around the holiday period.

Other religious traditions include the August 15 celebration of Mary, the virgin mother of Jesus. In villages and towns throughout Greece, at churches large and small, gatherings of the faithful often include processions through the streets.

Death and funerals are often part of religious traditions, and that's true in Greece, too. Women might wear black for a year after the death of a particularly close relative, while men don black armbands. A memorial service is usually held 40 days after the funeral to once again remember the deceased.

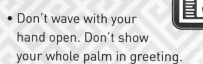

When in Greece...

- Don't wave with your hand open. Don't show your whole palm in greeting.
- Don't wear shorts while visiting one of the many churches. It is considered disrespectful. Women are also expected to cover their arms.
- An old superstition says that you should not stare too long at children, as they may think you are giving them the "evil eye."

National Customs

Birthdays are a big part of many cultures. However, in Greece, the name day of the saint from which a person gets his or her name is the big holiday.

The Greek Independence Day is celebrated each March 25. It marks the country's final separation from the Ottoman Empire.

During an Orthodox wedding service, the bride and the groom are "crowned" as a symbol of the "kingdom" that their marriage will be.

Each October 28 is Ohi Day. On that day in 1940, the leader of Greece at the time, the dictator Ioannis Metaxas, did not let Italians enter the country during the early days of World War II. Ohi means "No."

While Friday the 13th is considered unlucky in many Western countries, in Greece, locals are wary of any Tuesday the 13th.

And you know how when two people say something at the exact moment, there are some fun traditions (some Americans say, "You owe me a Coke," for instance)? In Greece when this happens, the phrase is *piase kokkino*, which means "touch red." So both people who spoke scramble to find anything red to touch to avoid bad luck!

Spitting in public is generally frowned upon, but in Greece, it can sometimes be a way to ward off bad luck. Hearing bad news—or even good news—can make some traditional Greeks make a short, triple spitting noise. The action is said to chase away the devil!

Do people at Greek celebrations still smash plates? That was for many decades a loud and expensive tradition. It was officially outlawed in 1969, but can sometimes be found at private events. Others try to carry on the tradition by throwing flowers.

As shown in the subject of a popular movie (*My Big Fat Greek Wedding*, 2002), Greek weddings might be familiar to American audiences. They are huge celebrations, packed with tradition. In the church, along with rings, the couple are given crowns to wear. The entire assembly kisses the couple before leaving the church. The receptions are packed with great food, traditional music, and dancing by everyone.

In all of their customs, Greeks emphasize family, tradition, and, often, a good time. *

At a Greek wedding

 GREECE

TiME TO EAT!

I just love the way they cook octopus in taverns.

YES...OCTOPUS!

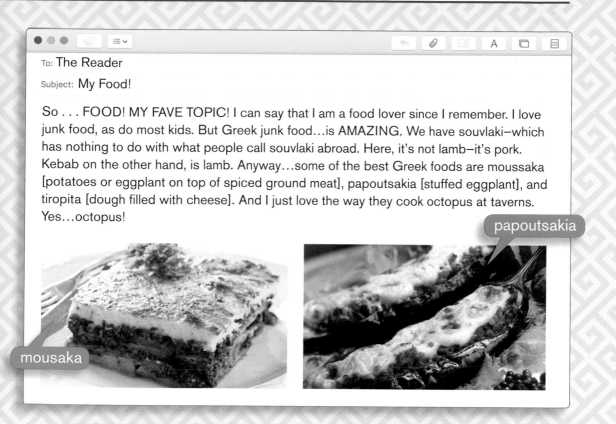

To: The Reader

Subject: My Food!

So . . . FOOD! MY FAVE TOPIC! I can say that I am a food lover since I remember. I love junk food, as do most kids. But Greek junk food...is AMAZING. We have souvlaki—which has nothing to do with what people call souvlaki abroad. Here, it's not lamb—it's pork. Kebab on the other hand, is lamb. Anyway...some of the best Greek foods are moussaka [potatoes or eggplant on top of spiced ground meat], papoutsakia [stuffed eggplant], and tiropita [dough filled with cheese]. And I just love the way they cook octopus at taverns. Yes…octopus!

papoutsakia

mousaka

SOUP'S ON (OR OFF!) We have soups like faki, fasolada, patsas, revithia, and trahanas. Mageiritsa [right] is a traditional soup made with lamb offal (the inside parts) and thickened with avgolemono (a sauce made with egg yolk and lemon juice) and we eat it the night of Greek Easter's Eve. I can tell you that it isn't everyone's favorite food, however. I can't even stand to smell it, but my mom says that it is really tasty.

TiME TO EAT!

 Hara Adams
My Daily Grub
Like • Comment • Share

Breakfast–For breakfast we drink a frappé or we eat pastries such as sweet mpougatsa, tiropita, spanakopita (pictured), or mpougatsa filled with something else (meat, spinach, cheese, etc.), and we drink chocolate milk.

Lunch–For lunch we eat Greek food made by mom or even me. You can pick from any of the dishes I already mentioned and you'll find something we like! My favorite meal is pita with gyros and tirokauteri, a spread made from cheese, peppers, and spices.

Desserts–We also have amazing sweets: baklavas (pictured at left), diples, sweet mpougatsa, oukoumades, and pasteli.

SNACKS! Mezedes are salads, spreads, and dips such as tirokauteri, tzatziki, taramosalata, skordalia, Greek salad (yes, that's a thing!), fried kolokithakia, Florina peppers, feta cheese, and so on.

NOT JUST GREEK

I've tried to eat Chinese food twice, but it didn't work for me. I do like McDonald's though, once in a while. I really love Italian food and I am not talking only about pizza. They have amazing cuisine. I have also tried Mexican food once and it was good enough for me. I could eat it again for sure.

Greek Culture

At one point in history, perhaps more than 2,000 years ago, Greek culture was one of the dominant forces in Western Europe. Its language was spoken by educated people in many countries, and its philosophy and literature were widely studied. Though it has been surpassed by others over the centuries, its influence remains and can be seen around the world.

Language

This ancient language grew from several strands that began more than 3,500 years ago. By the time of the power of the Athens city-state, the dialect used there of what had become Greek became the dominant version of the language. The language spread around the Mediterranean in part thanks to early Christians. They needed a single language that many people would understand, and Greek fit the bill. Many of the writings of St. Paul, for instance, that make up the New Testament were originally written in Greek. Most experts think the four Gospels were also first written down

Words to Understand

dialects   versions of a major language spoken by a smaller number of people

luster   shine, nice appearance, importance

mosaics   artwork created by forming tiny bits of colored tile into scenes, faces, and designs

in a form of Greek called *Koine*, or common. (For centuries in Western education, especially in Europe, learning Greek and Latin were a regular part of university educations. All Christian scholars had to learn both to read their Gospels in the original language.)

The influence of Alexander the Great spread Greek farther. Alexander learned it from his famous teachers and as his armies conquered new lands, he brought the language with him. The long period of Ottoman Turkish control over Greece halted the spread of the language, which continued to develop within Greece itself. One of the biggest issues was the use of a classical form in writing and another form in speaking.

By the time of the nationhood of Greece in the mid-1800s, a single form had become dominant, but there was still controversy over **dialects** and standards. In 1976, a single Greek language known as *dimotiki* was made the official national standard.

Greek, then as now, uses a different alphabet than English and the Romance languages (such as French or Italian). In fact, the word alphabet comes from the first two letters of Greek, alpha and beta.

Greek in English

Perhaps only Latin has had as much of an impact on what English is today as Greek has had. Estimates of how many Greek-influenced words are part of English run to more than 150,000. As the most common language of modern Europe for hundreds of years, Greek helped form English. A very short list of examples includes gymnasium, philosophy, economy, microscope, and idol. Many suffixes and prefixes are also from Greek roots. Look online to find some sayings based in Greek history, such as "Achilles' heel."

Art in Greece

Along with language, ancient Greece gave the world a great tradition of sculpture and design. For centuries, even after ancient Greece's heyday, people around the world were inspired by the busts, statues, and buildings

As Greece struggled with its economy, it got some good news in 2016 with the opening of a new National Museum of Contemporary Art.

made by artists of that period. The influence of these classical styles was hard to shake off, even as artistic styles changed over the centuries. When the Ottomans took over, they brought their own traditions, including **mosaics** and the making of icons for use in Orthodox churches. The creation of the modern, independent Greek state in 1822 opened up new avenues for artists. They brought influence from other European styles. They looked to contemporary Greek scenes for their subjects, which showcased everyday Greek life as well as the struggle for independence. Theodoros Vrizakis was one of the most well known Greek painters of this era.

In 2016, modern and contemporary Greek artists got a new showcase with the opening in Athens of the National Museum of Contemporary Art (EMST, an acronym based on the name in Greek).

Music and Dance

Greek music is enjoyed worldwide, which makes sense since its origins are many. The folk song traditions that were born many hundreds of years ago later added influences from the Ottomans and other parts of Europe. The idea that music should tell stories is a big part of traditional Greek songs. *Akritic* songs are more than 1,000 years old, from the Byzantine period. *Klephtic* songs are more recent, coming from the time of the independence of Greece. Each tells a kind of story that has been passed down for generations.

Some of the instruments have also been handed down. Greek music often calls for string instruments like a lute or the guitar-like bouzouki, as well as a type of bagpipe called a *tsabouna*.

Most regions in Greece boast unique folks dances, along with costumes that have been passed down through the centuries.

Fancy Dress

Greeks usually dress as most Europeans do, but they sometimes bring out traditional garb for special occasions. The presidential guardsmen known as Evzones, for example, wear a kilt-like skirt called a *fustanella*. They wear this over leggings and under a shirt with large, puffy sleeves. Their shoes sport tassels and are called *tsarouhia*. Watching them march is a popular tourist attraction in Athens.

Many modern Greek musicians and song-writers look to these ancient traditions for inspiration. They use the classical forms but add modern twists such as rock or jazz rhythms.

Much of this music also inspired a dance tradition. Each region has its own variations of Greek dance, but no Greek celebration is complete without a large group performance. Most dances are done in a circle, with dancers holding hands or holding ends of a handkerchief. They are seen as a celebration of the life and the time spent together with family and friends.

Food

Greek food is well known to just about any American, with most cities boasting at least one Greek restaurant. Greek food often includes olives of one kind or another. The fruit is grown throughout the country, and olive oil is one of its most important products. The nation's location on the sea means that seafood is often a part of meals. Its long farming tradition also has brought many vegetables onto the menu, including eggplant and artichokes. Lamb is a popular meat dish. The gyro (YEE-roh) sandwich is a familiar site at many American fairs or street scenes. Seasoned beef or lamb is roasted and carved off a spit and put into a pita along with lettuce, tomato, and yogurt-based tzatziki sauce.

The sweet known as loukoumades *are sort of like donut holes, sugary and covered with honey, but usually eaten as a dessert.*

Greek desserts are often laden with honey and often include the thin dough known as phyllo. And if you have a sweet tooth, a honey-drenched doughnut called a *loukoumades* will make your mouth water. (See Hara's descriptions of food for more information, page 30.)

Sports

Athens was the site of the first Olympic Games in 776 BCE. The modern Olympics were first held in Athens in 1896, inspired by those ancient Games. The modern Games were held in Athens again in 2004. Greece is one of only four nations that have been a part of every modern Summer Olympic Games, and sports remains a big part of Greek life.

As in most of Europe, soccer is the most popular sport, played and watched by people across Greece. One of the greatest moments in modern Greek sports history came in 2004, when the national team was the surprise winner of the European Championship. There has been a national soccer league since the early 1900s. In 2006, the Greek Superleague became the top level of pro soccer in the country; in 2017, it had almost two dozen teams. The Olympiacos FC team, based in Piraeus, has won the most national championships in the sport, with 29 through 2016.

Greece's national soccer team remains a source of pride. Here, team members celebrate after a big win gave them a place in the 32-team 2014 World Cup.

Basketball is a close second in popularity. A 14-team pro league plays throughout Greece. Thanks to the ongoing economic crisis (see chapters on Economy and on the Future), the Greek pro league has lost some of its **luster**. In the past, former NBA players from the United States would often play there. With the money in Greece disappearing, however, that is now much more rare, and players come mostly from Europe. In 2016, former Greek pro player Giannis Antetokounmpo signed a four-year contract for $100 million to continue his fine play in the United States for the Milwaukee Bucks of the NBA, who drafted him in 2013.

The NBA's "Greek Freak"

As the nation is nearly surrounded by water, sailing and windsurfing are popular pursuits for many people. ✶

GREECE

HARA'S TOWN

To: **The Reader**

Subject: **My Beautiful City!**

We LOVE Thessaloniki. We live in the best city in Greece, in my opinion. We don't live downtown, but we live a few minutes out of the center of Thessaloniki, or how we like to call it, Salonika.

It's beautiful here. The White Tower (left), the port, the coastal road, the cafeterias, the Aristotelous Square—everything. It's a place that never sleeps and there are always things to do. You never get bored and if someone visits Thessaloniki he falls in love with everything, even the alleys. And plus it's a city of love, either you are already in love or you are falling in love.

WE LOVE SALONIKA!

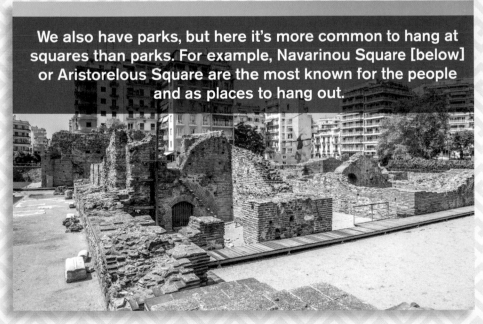

We also have parks, but here it's more common to hang at squares than parks. For example, Navarinou Square [below] or Aristorelous Square are the most known for the people and as places to hang out.

GREECE

HARA'S FREE TIME

To: The Reader

Subject: Working Out!

About my free time. I can tell that I didn't have enough of it this year but I made it work. I have been doing karate since I was four years old, and I do have a black belt. I compete at championships now, and I am doing very well.

My Music!
I do not have favorite kind of music. I listen to:
Greek
pop
hip-hop
rock
punk rock
old-school rock
r&b
tsiftetelia*
that's a kind of Middle Eastern music!

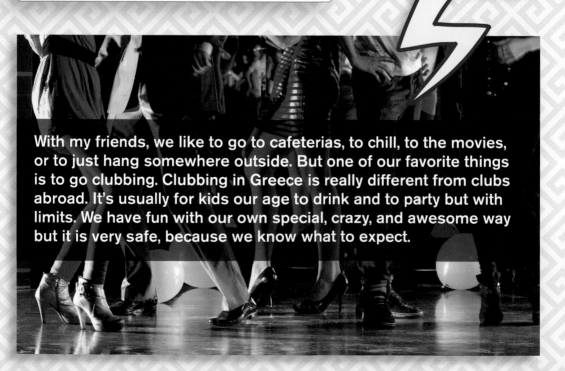

With my friends, we like to go to cafeterias, to chill, to the movies, or to just hang somewhere outside. But one of our favorite things is to go clubbing. Clubbing in Greece is really different from clubs abroad. It's usually for kids our age to drink and to party but with limits. We have fun with our own special, crazy, and awesome way but it is very safe, because we know what to expect.

To: The Reader

Subject: Just Hanging Out

What do we do when we hang out? We talk about how our classes went and that kind of stuff (don't tell that to my mother, too, but sometimes we smoke . . . ha-ha). But the best days are those we go on "field trips" outside our schoolyard. For us here in Greece, it's very common to just hang in the yard all day doing nothing (most of the time we just go for coffee).

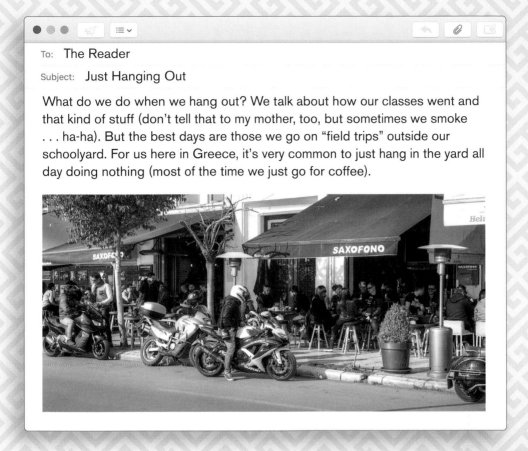

I do not have a part-time job but most of the teenagers I know do work. They usually work as waiters or at bakery shops or whatever anybody finds. I will look for a job after summer so I can earn my own money.

 GREECE

Greek Economy
and Politics

How do Greeks work and make money? In recent years, the answer to both parts of that question was "not much." Since 2008, Greece has been suffering from an extended financial crisis. The **European Union** (EU), the organization of continental countries, has repeatedly had to give Greece money to "stay in business." The World Bank, headquartered in Washington DC, has also had to step in to rescue Greece.

Words to Understand

austerity   a condition of living on very limited means and resources

coalition   a gathering of like-minded people or groups that gather for a common purpose

deficit   the difference between what a country take in as revenue and what it pays out as expenses; a deficit means it is more of the latter than the former

European Union   the organization that unites countries in Europe in a political and economic force

ratified   successfully voted into action

Like most countries in Europe, Greece uses the Euro as its currency. However, the 2000s brought chaos to the Greek economy, threatening its use of the Euro.

The Hectic 2000s

In 2008, a major worldwide economic crisis hit. Stock prices in many countries fell, especially in the US. The US real estate market collapse was another cause of the problem, but the effects of the problems were far reaching. In Europe, several countries saw their economies take big hits due to over-borrowing. That is, people, companies, and countries were borrowing too much money and then when revenue fell in the crisis, they could not pay it all off.

Greece was hit hardest of all by this problem. Its government continued to spend much more money than it took in. It also was not telling the whole truth and, in 2009, revealed that its **deficit** was much larger than

Olives, whether for use in oil or as the fruit alone, are a huge export crop for Greece.

be very productive. Cotton and tobacco are among the key crops. The most famous Greek product is olives. They are used as food, turned into oil, and canned or packaged for export. Other fruit, such as oranges and melons, are also successful crops. The nation also has a growing grape and wine industry.

Light Industry

One problem with having few large cities and lots of farmland is that Greece does not have a large number of factories or manufacturing. Among European Union countries, it has the third-lowest percentage of industry as part of its economy. There are no large auto or electronics industries, for example, which are huge parts of other countries' economies. Processing the food from farms—that is, turning the farm products into packaged or canned food—is one of the biggest parts of Greek industry, and that does not make nearly as much money as making cars. However, Greece's ancient tradition as a farming nation continues to help its economy.

Greece does have a record of success in refining petroleum. Oil pumped from the ground has to be refined into products for use, such as gasoline and kerosene. Greece buys oil from Russia and other nations and then refines it, selling the results to other countries. Turkey is a major customer for Greek refineries.

All those areas of business and more, however, depend on a stable government to help them stay healthy. And in recent years, that has not been the case.

Greek Government

Greece became an independent nation for the first time in 1822. It was recognized by European nations in 1830. Greece has had several constitutions over the years, but the one **ratified** in 1975 remains in force.

Greece is run by a Parliament elected by the people. The members of the leading party choose the prime minister, the main leader of the nation. Greece also has a president, but the role is mostly for official ceremonies. Greece, like other parliamentary nations, has a large number of political parties. Many are on the extreme left, or liberal, side of issues. Often in an election, one party will not get a majority in the Parliament, so several similar parties will band together to form a **coalition**. This group will then direct the moves Parliament makes.

In 1981, Greece became part of the EU. This group of countries agreed to open, for the most part, borders among themselves. In 2002, Greece joined EU members who were using a single European currency, the Euro. That relationship at first brought new investment and prosperity to Greece. Since the 2008 crisis, the relationship has soured as some EU nations do not appreciate having to prop up Greece. This will be a story to watch in the years to come. ✳

Greek debt crisis

HARA'S COUNTRY

To: The Reader

Subject: My Country

About the situation in my country, I have to say that it doesn't affect only my family but all of us. The problem isn't only economic but it's also social. I don't deal with politics any more. I think it's pointless. But luckily Greek people don't need money to have fun. A Greek man will have the same kind of fun with 100 Euros or with 2 Euros but the thing is that our problem is not how we will have fun. The problem is how families survive every month. Honestly, I believe almost everything in this country is damaged. And everyone thinks that we [the people] are responsible for this, but it's not us—it's our politicians. I know we vote for them but think what would happen if we didn't have politicians at all. We don't have a choice. It's really bad and sad that the country that gave birth to democracy now cannot handle it!

I really worry about the future 'cause I love my country but if I see I can't deal with the situation here, I will go abroad. Not only for me, but to help my family and my kids when and if I ever have any.

What Happened to Greece?

There is really not much to say . . . only that is very sad the fact that we are a country that created values such as democracy and now some people who happen to have power manipulate those values to earn money. I think that affects us all. They have harmed Greece's reputation and her quality of life, too.

There are some words in Greek like *filotimo* and *tsipa*. When we say someone has *filotimo* or *tsipa*, it means he is very honest, has pride and more—only a Greek man knows what exists behind those words. And that's sad. Because the same men who know the meaning of those words destroyed that country . . . MY country. For them to gain more and more and more money! And there are people who don't have homes anymore, because they took them. Not only my family has less, everybody has less, for them to have more. Those people disgust me.

I am just afraid for my parents, my brother and my future kids. I don't want them to live in that country, where everything is broken. And I am just tired of being afraid, because I don't know what will happen tomorrow. They are MAD, I am telling you. They don't give a [care] about us, the people. They just want more and more and more money and then they ask for more.

The Future of Greece

As noted in the previous chapter, Greece faces an uncertain future. Its economy is in bad shape, though many people are working to find a solution. Whether they succeed will determine that future for Hara and all the Greek people.

Corruption

One of the effects of the crisis was to shine a bright spotlight at a long-standing problem in Greece. For decades, the people at the top levels of government made sure that their friends and families got the best deals. Contracts were given to friendly companies instead of making sure the right people got them. "Who you know" became much more important than what you could contribute or produce. As the crisis grew, this web of

Words to Understand

reformers   people working to make fundamental changes in an organization or a society

As the debt crisis raged, large protests filled the streets calling for reform and answers, as here in Hara's hometown of Thessaloniki.

connections made it hard for **reformers** to make many changes. When the EU demanded that the government cut costs in order to obtain loans, many people in that web fought hard to make sure their area did not get cut. As a result, not enough cuts were made and the spiral continued. Reducing the amount of corruption in government will be vital to a more stable Greece.

Rotating Ministers

The way that Parliaments elect their leaders is different than in the United States, where elections are scheduled well in advance. In parliamentary countries such as Greece, new elections can be called at just about any time. If the coalition breaks down or if the prime minister becomes unpopular, a new election can be held to change things. For Greece, that has meant several elections in recent years. Each time, a new government has to form and get to work. All those changes make finding a long-lasting solution difficult.

In 2015, in fact, the Greek people elected a party called Syriza that was clearly against the EU requests to cut spending. By putting this party in charge, the government and the people seemed to be telling the people trying to help them that they didn't want any help. However, the Syriza government did make moves to cut spending in order to keep the EU loans coming.

Syrian Refugee Crisis

As if Greece were not hard-hit enough, in 2015 a new problem hit its shores, literally. An ongoing civil war in Syria, across the Mediterranean Sea from Greece, was sending millions of people fleeing the danger. Starting 2011, millions of people filled camps in Jordan, Lebanon, Turkey, and other nations close to Syria.

In 2015, the refugee flow increased, and many tried to cross the Mediterranean in boats to land in Greece, from where they wanted to go to other European countries. Though some nations, notably Germany, said they would accept some refugees, soon the flow became too great. At first, Greek army troops forced the refugees away or took them back to other countries. Over time, though, Greek islands became refugee camps, filled with people looking for safety. More Syrians reached Greece through Turkey in the northern part of the country. In spring 2016, a deal between Turkey and Greece helped stop the largest flow of the refugees from coming to Greece. However, the refugees are still in crisis, and many are stuck in Greece, so this situation is not resolved, by any means.

Greece remains a flashpoint in the ongoing refugee crisis, as people from the Middle East and other places try to flee to safety in Europe.

What's Next

As Hara writes on page 52, the future of Greece is uncertain. Over the past decade or so, the country has not yet been able to find a way out of its economic problems. The longer they pile up, the harder they will be to solve. The impact of the government not having enough money will have a ripple effect that will be hard to stop. The government doesn't seem to have the answers, and the people are stuck with hard choices about what to do with limited money.

Looming over Athens is the ancient Parthenon, symbol of a long-ago age when Greece was truly great. Will it find a way to become great again?

In the coming years, Greeks will continue to struggle with having enough money, both for themselves and as a nation. They will have to make do with less, which is always hard. They also have to find a way to get a government in place that will make the hard choices but also convince the people to go along with them. One solution might be to leave the "Eurozone," the area that uses the Euro currency. No one wants that to happen, though, so it's probably a last resort.

However, Greece has one of the longest and proudest histories in the world. The Greeks connect themselves to their ancient relatives on a daily basis. Through all the centuries, the Greek people are, if anything, devoted to each other and their country. Their culture and their spirit will play a huge part in finding a solution to the problems of today. ✳

Greece's future

 GREECE

 # TEXT-DEPENDENT QUESTIONS

1. What does the word "democracy" mean?

2. What empire took over Greece starting in the 1200s?

3. What is the name of the dominant Christian denomination in Greece?

4. What fruit is a major export as well as a big part of Greek food?

5. In your own words, explain the Greek financial crisis.

6. In what area of business is Greece a major world leader?

7. From what country did refugees come to Greece starting in 2015?

RESEARCH PROJECTS

1. See if you can make a list of 25 English words that come from Greek roots. Try without looking them up first to see how many you already know!

2. Make a chart that connects the major ancient Greek philosophers. Who studied with whom? What were some of their key beliefs? How did they influence later thinkers?

3. Time to eat! Find a recipe for a Greek dish and see if you can make it with your friends. *Yassou*! (That means "Cheers!" in Greek.)

4. Research some of the popular Greek islands to which many people go as tourists. Pick your favorite and design a poster encouraging people to go there.

FIND OUT MORE

Books

Cahill, Thomas. *Sailing the Wine-Dark Sea: Why the Greeks Matter*. New York: Anchor Books, 2004.

Riordan, Rick. *Percy Jackson and the Olympians*. New York: Disney-Hyperion, 2005. (Note: This is the first in a popular series of novels based on the ancient Greek myths.)

Williams, Jean Kinney. *Empire of Ancient Greece (Great Empires of the Past)*. New York: Chelsea House, 2009.

Websites

www.cia.gov/library/publications/the-world-factbook/geos/gr.html
Read more about Greece on this site from the US government's CIA.

www.educationworld.com/a_lesson/explaining-the-greek-economic-crisis-with-students.shtml
A good discussion of the Greek economic crisis.

www.visitgreece.gr/
Find out more about visiting Greece on this official site from the Greek government.

SERIES GLOSSARY OF KEY TERMS

arable land   land suitable for cultivation and the growing of crops

commodity   a raw material that has value and is regularly bought and sold

cuisine   cooking that is characteristic of a particular country, region, or restaurant

destabilize   damage, disrupt, undermine

dynasties   long periods of time during which one extended family rules a place

industrialization   the process in which an economy is transformed from mainly agricultural to one based on manufacturing goods

infrastructure   buildings, roads, services, and other things that are necessary for a society to function

lunar calendar   a calendar based on the period from one moon to the next. Each cycle is 28 1/2 to 29 days, so the lunar year is about 354 days

parliamentary   describes a government in which a body of cabinet ministers is chosen from the legislature and act as advisers to the chief of state (or prime minister)

resonate   echo and reverberate; stay current through time

sovereignty   having supreme power and authority

venerate   treat with great respect

INDEX

Photo Credits

Adobe Images: Arena Creative 32t. Alamy Stock: Photo12 18. Christos Was Here: 8, 20, 26, 42r. Dreamstime. com: Niklas Ramberg 9b, castenoid 9r, joyfull 10, Panagiotis Karapanagiotis 13, Aleksandr Kamasi 15, Nexus7 16, Dimaberkut 17, 25, GVictoria 21t, Antoniodiaz 21b, Kostyantin Pankin 22t, Vassilis Anastasiou 22c, Verkoka 22b, Lucian Milasan 23l, Rigmanyi 23r, Piotr Marcinski 27, Robert Lerich 30, HiPhoto 31l, Dvalmas 31r, Athina Psoma 31b, Bhofack2 32c, jabiru 32b, Dinoforiena 33t, Konstantin Zemenov 33c, Michael Zhang 33b, Eleni Seitandiou 37, Diamantis Seitandis 38, Sergii Koval 39, Cosmin Iftode 40, Leonid Andronov 42l, Milosk50 43b, Piotr290 43t, 45t, Alen Ciric 44t, Pitangacherry 44b, Zimmytws 47, Petros Tsonis 49, Inacio Pires 50, Kpikoulas 52, Diamantis Seitandis 55, Anjo Kan 57, Joop Kleuskens 59. iStock: ImageSource 23b. Newscom: Georgios Georgiou/Zuma Press 36. Shutterstock: IVashstudio 28, Kemih 45b.

Author

James Buckley Jr. is a veteran writer of books for young and adult readers. He is the author of numerous biographies in the popular "Who Was…?" series, along with many books from Scholastic on sports. He thanks his good friend Dr. Nick Rose for helping him connect with Hara.